N+B

A GUIDE
TO
BASIC
RIDING
INSTRUCTION

1·2·

2

wld

A GUIDE
TO
BASIC
RIDING
INSTRUCTION

Anne Lewis
Illustrated by the author

J A ALLEN : LONDON

ISBN 0 85131 218 7

Published in 1975 by J.A. Allen & Company Limited,
1 Lower Grosvenor Place, Buckingham Palace Road,
London, SW1W 0EL

Set IBM 10/12 Press Roman by
Specialised Offset Services Limited, Liverpool
Printed and bound by The Devonshire Press Ltd., Torquay.

CONTENTS

PREFACE

On the subject of riding, there seem to be any number of books concerning what to teach but not how to teach it. I have the impression that many young riding instructors are thrown in at the deep end, so to speak, and it is to try and ease their lot that I have written the following chapters.

Some of what I have written might be considered controversial; if so, that is all to the good. Controversial ideas can be helpful to anyone who is in the process of forming his own opinions and developing his own personal method of instructing.

As this book deals with the 'how' of teaching, rather than the 'what', it is suggested that it is read in conjunction with the B.H.S. *Manual of Horsemanship* and *The Instructors Handbook*.

Chapter 1

LEAD IN

When I went off, newly qualified, to my first job as a riding instructor in a boarding school in the north of Scotland, my head was full of the basic rules of instructing. I had passed the instructional section of the examination partly because I had been able to tell my ride that the trot was a diagonal pace of two-time and that there were two ways of riding the trot, and so on. I had explained, demonstrated, had the ride practising, explained the faults beginners are prone to, demonstrated these and explained how to overcome them. I knew it all from the book.

My first batch of riders at the school, boys of twelve to fourteen years old, were, I was told, 'our best riders'. They all looked good and when I had them going round as a ride, they were hard to fault. Then I lined them up in the centre of the manège and asked each one, in turn, to walk his pony out onto the track and ride round on his own. Not one could leave the ride.

This was my first awakening. So where was I? According to the book, pupils should learn, gradually, to ride at all paces and all the time be improving their control and influence on the horse. I was about to say this was where I threw the book out of the window, but in fact I never did that. I had had the basics drummed into me by that Master, the late Dick Pritchard and there is no doubt that those basics will always apply.

It was simply that I learned early on that it is often necessary to adapt to the particular circumstances, place, people, horses, in which and with whom one finds oneself. I merely laid the book aside, as it were, whilst keeping the basics firmly in mind. I found that in my time at that school I had to adapt my teaching to suit the youth and varied ability of my pupils. Having adopted my own method and used it for three years, I was in for another rude awakening.

In my own training I had learned all about the various reins and their uses — indirect rein of opposition in front of the withers, and so on. At the boarding school I had taught the more advanced of my ten-to-fourteen-year-olds how to use some of these reins but never the names of them. My main purpose had been to try and develop 'feel' in the children and as they were not potential riding instructors, I had filled their heads with as few technicalities as possible. After three years I decided it was time to get back into the swim, because there was very little 'horse' activity in the north of Scotland at that time. I went for an interview for a post instructing pupils for the first of the British Horse Society examinations in a large residential riding school in England. At the interview I was given a rather gassy little horse to ride, one which preferred not to go into the corners of the school.

After a little while I achieved some success and was asked, 'What rein did you use to get him into the corners?'

I went completely blank. 'E'em — this one' I said, and showed the lady.

'Yes, but what's it *called*?'

'Oh,' I said, 'I'm afraid I've forgotten all the names.'

Well, I did get the job, but I was told (not unnaturally, I thought), that I should need to do some revision before starting to teach the examination candidates.

This rather long-winded story is merely to illustrate how adaptable a riding instructor has to be. So rarely is everything ideal. So often he is faced with a ride consisting of people of varying ability, some of whom ride perhaps two or three times a week and some two or three times a month. He will have to provide instruction which will suit both groups at the same time. More often than not, the horses he has at his disposal will be far from ideal. He may have some that buck, some which bite or kick other horses and some which are hopelessly sluggish; more often than not most of them will be so lacking in suppleness that they cannot be expected to give novice riders the right 'feel'.

Perhaps one of the most important lessons a young instructor has to learn is that he must be prepared to offer something quite different to each pupil who comes his way. For example, he must realise that whereas a keen, competent young rider who has ridden for years may revel in being driven hard and perhaps even bawled at, a nervous adult beginner merely needs his confidence built up at first and any bawling, at him, would probably drive him away from riding for good.

He should try to understand his pupils' aims. Is this child with his own pony which is really too much for him the victim of over-keen, pushing parents? Does that thirty-year-old housewife merely want to learn to sit safely on a quiet horse out hacking, so she can get some exercise and keep her weight down? Does this apparently terrified eight-year-old really want to learn to ride or is she just trying to keep up with her two older sisters? If he knows the answers to questions such as these he will find it much easier to know what to give such people.

An instructor is normally a keen rider himself and finds it hard to understand how anyone else can be anything but fascinated by his subject; but he must accept the fact that they can, and not ram his enthusiasm down his pupils' throats. Pupils with the same degree of keenness as the enthusiastic, dedicated instructor are, of course, a joy to teach and make it all seem worthwhile. Nevertheless, there is undoubtedly satisfaction to be gained from teaching, for example, the nervous beginner — building up his confidence and showing him that every time he rides he can take at least one step forward.

An instructor may teach a large number of people in any one day, but he should remember that to each person, this is his one hour, perhaps one lesson, in a week. He should receive value for money and feel that the instructor has done his best for him. He should go away looking forward to his next lesson because he has enjoyed this one and feels he has achieved something.

Chapter 2

QUALITIES OF AN INSTRUCTOR

This chapter consists of a selection of qualities which I think one would like to find in the ideal riding instructor. I have yet to meet this ideal but I have met several who come close to it. Throughout, I speak of 'he', because to say 'he or she' on every occasion would make very tedious reading.

He must love his subject, have a good knowledge of it and be an able horseman himself.

Most of this is obvious; no one can teach well if he dislikes his subject and knows very little about it, but it is debatable whether a riding instructor needs to be an exceptional horseman. Everyone knows that the most brilliant people in their particular field are, with exceptions, often the poorest teachers. Such people may find it hard to suffer fools gladly, consequently they are unlikely to be able to help and encourage people who are very much less able than they are themselves. With riding, so long as the knowledge is there, it is sufficient if the instructor is only a reasonably competent rider himself, certainly at the lower levels. Many people may disagree with this, but given a gifted teacher who is a moderate horseman only, and a brilliant horseman with none of the gifts of a teacher, I think it is the former who will get the best results as an instructor.

He must have patience and self-control.

Many of us have had lessons from instructors who lack these qualities, but only the most keen riders will be content to continue to take lessons from them.

Sometimes very great self-control is needed. There will probably be many occasions when, in a state of exasperation, an instructor will ask himself why a certain pupil bothers to go on riding — 'he doesn't seem to want to learn and he has absolutely no talent.' But the pupil is a paying client and the instructor had a duty towards him and must bite back his intolerant outburst.

An instructor should never lose his temper, but I believe there are occasions when he is justified in *using* it. From time to time, one comes across a 'know-all' who maltreats a horse, even if not particularly roughly; for the good of the horse and, one hopes, of other horses he may ride, it can help to cut such people down to size, occasionally. Also, although not everyone may agree, an occasional outburst of this kind gives the instructor the sort of reputation he wants; he will be regarded as someone who is in control of the situation. If it becomes known that he is not invariably placid and easy-going, he will be all the more respected.

He must have personality and confidence in his knowledge of the subject and his ability to put it across.

No little mouse will make a good instructor, therefore the stronger the personality, the better. He must be able to convince people that he knows what he is talking about. A touch of that 'something' which goes to make a good actor is often to be found in a good riding instructor.

He must have imagination.

This is necessary to enable him to have some understanding of how his pupil is feeling and also so that he is able, mentally, to ride his pupil's horse for him. Only this way is it possible to teach 'feel'.

He must like people, be kind and sympathetic, yet firm.

He must like people enough to ensure that he shows no favouritism; if he likes people he will be capable of finding the redeeming features of an outwardly unattractive personality. If he does *not* like people, he will not care whether he does his best for his pupils or not. He *must* care about this. He must be sufficiently sympathetic to be understanding about any difficulties or fears his pupils may have, but he must be firm enough to push them to greater effort, at times even a little beyond what they had thought was their limit.

He should have a sense of humour.

There are times when a sense of humour is invaluable. Pupils may become tense through trying too hard and unsuccessfully, and often at such times, a touch of humour to lighten the atmosphere relaxes everyone and things start to go right. But an instructor must laugh with, not at, his pupils.

He must be tactful.

There are various occasions when it is necessary to show tact. For example, a ride does not always consist of pupils of equal ability; it may be that there are one or two very able children in a ride with one or two much less able adults and tact may be needed in such a situation to prevent the latter losing face.

He should not be vain.

An instructor with excessive vanity will probably be someone who is over-fond of the sound of his own voice and too concerned with his own image to have his pupils enjoyment and progress at heart.

Chapter 3

GENERAL POINTS ON TAKING A LESSON

An instructor should always be neatly turned out. It is an insult to the pupils to give a lesson in an open-necked shirt and the jeans in which he did the mucking-out. It is better to be over-formal than the reverse. Currently many people seem to consider that instructors should wear hard hats. This seems to me unnecessary, though one should always have a hard hat available to wear whenever it is necessary to get onto a pupil's horse. I am assuming, above, that the instructor is on his feet. There are advantages in his being mounted but I think these are, except when taking advanced pupils, outweighed by the disadvantages. The main advantage is that he does not have to borrow someone's horse if he wants to give a demonstration. If the ride *does* consist of advanced pupils and the instructor has a well-trained horse at his disposal, then he should certainly be mounted himself, but otherwise, I think not. There is nothing worse than trying to instruct from the back of a horse that is playing up or refusing to stand still; besides, being a mounted instructor is quite an art and takes practice. Anyone who has not tried it may scoff at that statement but those who are in the habit of taking a ride on their feet may find it very difficult to sit still on a horse. This is especially true of those who, when not mounted, tend to use their hands as an extension of their voice to explain their meaning.

With a ride of novices, there is no doubt at all that one is better on one's feet. Ideally there should be a reasonably experienced rider as leading file, as this will make it much easier for the novices to keep their horses going — and going in the right direction; thus, when demonstrations are needed, the leading file can give them, with guidance from the instructor. Apart from the usefulness of this, it will make the leading file ride at his best, give him something to do and keep him interested when he would otherwise probably be very bored.

Another good reason for his being on his feet is that the instructor is able to walk over to a pupil and, physically, correct his basic position, or show him, for example, how to shorten his reins correctly or change his stick from one hand to the other. These things are well-nigh impossible from the back of a horse.

Always plan beforehand what you intend to cover in a lesson, even though you may, in the event, never get round to this chosen subject. Because of what develops during the lesson you may decide instead to work at some difficulty which has cropped up, or perhaps a pupil may ask you if the ride can work at a certain movement which they have previously found particularly difficult or confusing. So be prepared to be adaptable but always have something up your sleeve. There is nothing more obvious than an instructor who has run out of ideas, keeps looking at his watch and is quite clearly wondering how he can keep his pupils busy until the hour is up.

The easiest type of instructing is when taking a course, when a program is planned beforehand and fairly rigidly adhered to. The pupils will be the same people throughout and continuity is possible. The most difficult type of instructing is taking a once-a-week ride consisting of one or two who turn up every week and one or two who only manage once a fortnight. Add to this the fact that some are twice as experienced as the others and you have the typical ride many instructors are faced with, more often than not. This will test any instructor's flexibility and ingenuity.

. . . . there is nothing worse than trying to take a ride from the back of a horse that is playing up . . . .

Whatever you decide to teach, always keep in the front of your mind that the prime object should be the pupils' enjoyment. What constitutes enjoyment for one may be quite different from what constitutes enjoyment for another; one may only want to spend an hour plodding round the school on a horse's back while another is really keen to get on and learn. Somehow all tastes must be catered for.

I think it is fairly safe to say that the time spent by the instructor talking, while the pupils are stationary, should be directly related to the frequency of their lessons. If, for example, they are on a course and riding for two or three hours a day for a week or several weeks, explanations should be given while the pupils and horses rest. If they are novice riders, riding once a week, who will not, anyway, tax their horses unduly, all the time possible should be given to active riding, so that advantage is taken of almost every minute they are on a horse. This way they will progress faster and their riding muscles will have more change to develop.

Make sure that your voice is loud enough to be heard by everyone. Keep the sound of your voice interesting and not all at one level. Put life into it so that it will stimulate your pupils to make an effort.

Be sure to give commands in plenty of time so that aids are not hurriedly or roughly applied. If you are about to ask for something you are not sure everyone has done before, explain beforehand. For example, 'In a moment I shall be asking each of you to trot round the school individually to the back of the ride. I shall say 'Leading files in succession, trot and take the rear of the ride — leading file commence'. The rest of the ride will remain in walk.' They will then know what to expect.

Try to avoid going up to one pupil and speaking to him alone, except on the occasions when it is necessary with beginners.

Gear the level of your explanations to the ability of your ride. Do not fill people's heads with unnecessary technicalities in the early stages and with children, make every explanation as simple as possible. Because trainee instructors have to obtain experience, it is usually the practice in most establishments to put the novice riders in their hands. It is hard to see how this can be avoided but there are dangers in it. If beginners are not well taught, they may develop bad habits and wrong ideas early on which become very difficult to eradicate. Trainee instructors should be supervised as much as possible, for their own and the clients' good, and if possible novice riders should have an experienced instructor for the first two or three lessons and from time to time thereafter. Another of the dangers mentioned above is that, like an advanced car driver who is not experienced in teaching, a trainee riding instructor may try and teach novices advanced methods. I remember being horrified at an example of this once; a child pupil had reached the stage when she wanted to try her first canter and her instructor went into a detailed explanation for the aids for a left canter.

Always try to ensure that something is achieved by each pupil every time they are asked to do anything. Do not, for example, ask them to canter in succession to the rear of the ride, then say 'That was quite good', and leave it at that; say what was good and what was not. For example, 'That was very well prepared but you lost it just before the downward transition and your horse went onto his forehand'. Then when that same pupil is about to try again, say 'Now remember this time — stronger driving aids on the downward transition.'

Criticism must be constructive or little is likely to be achieved. It is useless to tell someone what he is doing wrong and omit to say what he should do to put it right.

Be sure to give praise but do not be too lavish with it.

Remember that praise should be related to effort not ability. An improvement or the correction of a fault, at any level, merits praise. There is no one more discouraging than the instructor who only comments on what the pupil does badly. If people have worked hard, however limited their ability, they should go away feeling at least a small sense of achievement and with a desire to come back and learn more.

Do not be deterred if you are confronted with a ride of very mixed ability, unless this is too extreme. It is impossible to give value for money if one pupil in a ride is at an advanced stage and another is having his second or third lesson. Inside such extremes it is not too difficult. So long as the least able pupil can keep his horse going forward at the same pace as the others and is not a complete passenger, a ride of mixed ability can be quite a good thing. You ask more of the advanced pupils than of the novices and the novices work harder to try and fit in and they get an idea of what will be expected of them at a later stage. The advanced pupils can also be used as demonstrators and this is good for anyone's self esteem.

Do not snatch every opportunity of getting onto a pupil's horse and showing him how good you are and how it *should* be done. Each time you contemplate doing this, ask yourself — Is it really necessary? If I am patient and let him keep trying, isn't he likely to succeed? Has he got the horse into such a state that he will never make it without help? Or is his failure due to a 'bolshie' horse which I should now get on and square up? Consider honestly and only ask him to make way for you if you are sure it is necessary.

Always try to finish each lesson on a good note. This is most important because the impression a pupil takes away with him will be influenced much more by how things went at the end than by any difficulties he may have encountered early in the lesson.

Lastly, keep an open mind. Remember that the best horsemen and instructors are those who, the more they learn, the more clearly they realise how little they know. Do not be bigoted. If a pupil voices an idea in opposition to what you have always believed, consider it carefully and if you cannot accept it, explain why. But there are times when pupils' ideas give one food for thought and shake some of one's long-held beliefs. Be prepared to modify your ideas and when possible, take lessons youself, however long ago you became a qualified instructor. It will give you fresh ideas about both riding and teaching, confirm your old ones (one hopes) and keep your riding up to scratch.

Chapter 4

THE THREE METHODS
OF TEACHING A BEGINNER

There are three ways of starting off beginners. They are:— on the lunge, on the leading rein, or free in an enclosed space.

Lunge.

Unquestionably this method will produce the most rapid progress, *if* the pupil is able to have a minimum of, say, three lessons a week for several weeks in succession. If he can only afford, in time or money, to have one or two lessons a week, this does not seem to me a good method. No one, whose muscles are not accustomed to the physical position of a rider on a horse, can comfortably endure more than about twenty minutes of it at a time, at first. An isolated twenty minutes, even twice a week, will mean very slow progress and will probably not bring with it any real feeling of achievement, nor will it do much towards developing the riding muscles.

For this method to be really successful, the pupil should ride every day. It is a good method because it makes it possible for the pupil to become familiar with the paces, to learn to go with the movement of the horse, to develop a deep and relaxed seat and all without having to concern himself with control. Because of this last, it is obviously necessary to have a horse which lunges well and calmly and has a gentle, even action, and an instructor who is capable of doing the job well. This involves not merely being able to get a horse to go round him and stop, but to keep the horse going round at an even pace, particularly in the 'lazy' trot which is the most desirable. He must also be capable, while doing this, of giving most of his attention to his pupil and being able to spot faults in his position as they arise.

I mentioned the lack of any need on the part of the pupil to try and control the horse. He would not, of course, have much idea how to try and do this anyway, if he had never ridden before, but the great thing about this method is that the riding muscles can be developed merely by the pupil being on a horse, in the correct position and also by the many helpful exercises he can be asked to do. The pupil who is not on the lunge will have to keep his horse going forward himself. Trying to keep in the correct position while using the legs *before* the riding muscles have developed is very difficult and almost invariably results in a loss of position and a weakening of the seat.

Someone who has spent several weeks having lessons on the lunge will become familiar with the horse's movements and will be confident and reasonably comfortable and well down in the saddle. Once he had passed the stage of needing to hold on the the saddle, riding with his hands free will have proved to him that he can keep his balance and go with the horse without clutching on to anything. This is a very big step towards acquiring an independent seat and one which is much slower to come to a pupil taught any other way.

When the time comes for him to ride a horse off the lunge he will be able to give most of his attention to the matter of control and not have to think too much about keeping his position.

Leading Rein.

Leading a pupil, first from the ground and later from another horse, is probably the best method for small children. With some riding schools, where there is no indoor school or manège, it is the *only* way for all pupils. For all but the small

.... *mounting without even holding the reins* ....

children I think it must be considered the least satisfactory method, principally because the instructor cannot see properly what his pupil is doing.

Free.

This is probably the most enjoyable way to learn — and to teach. With reliable, steady horses in an enclosed space it should be a perfectly safe method. Some instructors insist on having their beginners led for a very long time, but provided the horses are kind and do not try to take advantage of their riders, very little leading should be necessary. But have people available to lead, for a time.

One word of warning here. At most riding schools there are plenty of children only too willing to do this job but some of them may regard themselves as budding instructors, so brief them first, or you may find they are giving their own private lessons sotto voce, and not according to your methods, either.

Most beginners are a little apprehensive, naturally enough; a horse seems a very large creature to someone who is not accustomed to them. I have found that if, in their first lesson, they find they can stop and start of their own accord it does wonders for their confidence and gives them a real sense of achievement.

Whatever method of giving the initial lessons is adopted, insist on having things done the right way from the start. I have gone into the school to find pupils I have not previously taught, but to whom I was about to give their third of fourth lesson, trying to mount without even picking up the reins, because the finer points had been overlooked. If correct methods are insisted on from the very beginning they will become almost instinctive good habits. Bad habits can be very difficult to eradicate but as well as this, the correct methods are almost invariably the safe methods.

Chapter 5

BEGINNERS ON THE LUNGE

Only teach a pupil by this method if you have previously acquired sufficient skill at lunging a riderless horse to be able, when it has a rider, to give most of your attention to *him*.

Even if there are several suitable horses available for giving lessons on the lunge, it is as well to use the same one every time, for the first few lessons. Do not expect a beginner to get onto a horse which is on the lunge if it has just been brought out of the stable. Make sure you have ten minutes or so before your pupil arrives to lunge the horse without its rider. This enables the animal to settle down and allows you to check the adjustment of the tack, particularly the side-reins. Tack up the horse with the side-reins fixed to a snaffle bit; this can be either on its own bridle or attached to the cavesson, but do not fit any ordinary reins onto the bit.

In the later chapter about the first lesson free, in an enclosed space, I have advocated teaching the correct mounting method some way through the lesson, rather than at the beginning. I think the same applies here. Allow your possibly nervous pupil to have a chance to ride round at a walk first and get the feel of a horse, if he has never ridden before. When he has relaxed and is perhaps in need of a break from riding, teach him dismounting followed by mounting. Since everyone should learn how to receive a leg-up onto a horse, you can get him into the saddle that way when he first arrives.

The main advantage of lunging, as a method of learning, is that it is taught without reins and stirrups, but no one should be given the first three or four lessons entirely without stirrups or they may find themselves almost crippled with muscular

. . . . only teach a pupil by this method, if you have previously acquired sufficient skill . . . .

stiffness on the day following their first lesson. So start your pupil off with stirrups and take advantage of having them, to teach the correct method of adjusting them. This is another thing you can teach when your pupil and horse need a break.

Initially, a rider will probably feel more secure if he holds the pommel of the saddle with both hands, but very early on, insist that he holds the cantle with his inside hand and the pommel with his outside hand; this helps to keep his shoulders at right-angles to his horse's spine, which is how they should always be. In walk, he will probably not find it necessary to hold on at all, except perhaps for the first few moments of the first lesson. He will need to continue to hold the saddle for some time in trot, but when he begins to feel secure, he should cease to hold the cantle and only hold the pommel with his outside hand. The next step is to stop holding on at all, except when he feels in danger of losing his balance. Thereafter it is best for him to hold his hands in the position in which they would be when holding reins in the normal way. If he does this he will soon become accustomed to the correct position of the head, shoulders, arms and hands.

Most of the work is, of course, done in trot but remember that this will be very tiring at first and allow plenty of spells of walking in between short periods of trotting. To help check faults in position you will need someone else to come and assist you, at least once or twice during the lesson. If your assistant is a knowledgeable person he can stand behind and also to the outside of your pupil and tell you whether he is sitting squarely in the saddle and whether the position of his outside leg is correct. If your assistant is not capable of doing this but can manage to take over the lunging for a few moments, you can go and check yourself.

After the first few lessons, introduce short periods of riding without stirrups. On the first occasion, only ask for this in a walk and for the duration of a few simple exercises, but later on get your pupil to start trotting without stirrups. Whilst on the subject of exercises, lessons on the lunge should consist of about one third exercises. Gradually increase the duration of the periods without stirrups so that, by the fourth lesson or so, nearly the entire ride is without them and from about the fifth lesson, tack up the horse without any. When your pupil has been riding for a month or more and is relaxed and secure on the horses with smooth action which he has so far been riding, he can graduate to a horse with stronger action. In fact, at this stage he will benefit by riding a variety of horses.

Chapter 6

BEGINNERS ON THE LEADING REIN

As mentioned previously, early lessons on the leading rein are the least satisfactory method of teaching, though it is possible to achieve a good deal this way. If, through a lack of facilities, this is the method which *must* be adopted, the instructor should consider several things before deciding which horses to use. He should not, for example, try to lead a child on a 12 hand pony from a long-striding 16 hand hunter. The pony will only be able to walk three or four strides before it has to trot to catch up and this can be alarming and uncomfortable for a nervous beginner. Then, when the instructor's horse is trotting, the pony's trot will necessarily be so rapid that, if the poor child is learning to rise to the trot, he will not stand a chance. Be careful not to use two horses, or a horse and a pony, which do not get on well together. There is actual danger in this, because the pupil could receive a kick meant for his mount. But apart from the element of danger, even a playful attempt by one horse to bite the other can be a very alarming experience for a novice, even if simply because it causes sudden and unexpected movement.

Whilst not advocating the leading rein as a method of giving early lessons, I do think that there can come a time when to take a pupil out on the leading rein is the best thing to do. Sometimes, pupils who have had a number of lessons in a school or manège, reach the stage when they are convinced that they are no longer making progress. Perhaps, for example, after several lessons attempting it they still cannot achieve a rising trot. This can be due to a naturally poor sense of rhythm, or occasionally to bad instruction, but it is more

*. . . . consider several things before decid-
ing which horses to use . . . .*

likely to be caused by a pupil's trying too hard and not allowing himself to relax and feel. At such times a ride out will relax him, give him other things to think about and look at and he will realise he is not being watched all the time. If such a lesson is for this therapeutic purpose, the instructor will do well to talk about anything but riding most of the time. All this can be sufficient to make everything start going right, but even if it should prove not to help with one particular difficulty it will be a refreshing change from the hard slogging in a confined space. Hacking quietly through pleasant country in good weather will give a slow learner a preview of what he will be in a position to do when he has achieved greater proficiency and so provide a spur to his efforts.

Chapter 7

BEGINNERS IN THE SCHOOL OR MANÈGE - FIRST LESSON

The next six chapters consist of a possible program for the first six lessons for beginners. There is no suggestion that any trainee instructor should adhere rigidly to them; my aim is to supply ideas and point out possible pitfalls.

Let us assume that you have three adults in an indoor school, about to start their first lesson. Before actually starting on the lesson, I would like to digress on the subject of tacking up. At many riding schools, the horses are tacked up by the staff and taken from the clients to be un-tacked at the end of the ride. There are people who expect this, as part of the service for which they are paying and they are perfectly justified in this view. However, I have met many people who long to get to know horses in the stable and learn how to handle them and who would very much like to be able to tack up themselves. I think they should be allowed to do this, so long as they are prepared to arrive sufficiently early. A member of the staff will have to take the time to teach how it is done and then supervise for the first few attempts. Since an instructor should always check the tack of every horse in his ride anyway, before he starts a lesson, there should be no risk attached to the pupil doing the job himself. I think it should go without saying that the horses should have properly adjusted neck-straps and do not forget to explain to the pupils what they are for.

There are a number of elementary things which have to be taught to beginners, such as how to lead a horse, how to tighten the girth before mounting and how to mount. The

obvious time to teach these things is at the beginning but I
think it is preferable to leave them until the pupils have ridden
for a little while. Many beginners, much as they want to learn
to ride, are a bag of nerves when the time to get on the horse
actually arrives, simply because they do not know what to
expect in their early lessons. If this is the case they will not be
in a fit state to remember detailed explanations of anything.
So get them onto their horses, either with the simplest
explanation of the mounting procedure or by giving them a leg
up. Give the most simple instructions on how to sit, or none at
all if they seem to fall into a good natural position, adjust their
stirrups for them, show them how to hold the reins and then
let the assistants lead them round the school at a walk. This is
the time, if you had not previously done so, when you will
find out which of your pupils is nervous. Those who are not
will soon be sitting up in a relaxed manner, going easily with
the movement of the horse. Those who are will probably be in
a slightly crouched position with their muscles apparently
rigid. To these last it is time to say, smilingly, 'Unless anyone
particularly wants to see what a trot feels like, what is
happening now is the worst that will happen to you
today — so relax and enjoy it' — or something to that effect.

Once your pupils appear quite happy you can begin to
teach them. This is a good time to tell them, somewhat
sketchily, about the correct basic position, in fact merely the
basics of the basic position, because they will soon be trying
the accelerator and brakes and they must not be asked to
think about too many things at once. Ask the assistants to
turn in and halt the horses, then explain to the pupils that
they should sit erect but supple, and squarely in the middle of
the saddle on both seat bones. Make sure that the leg position
is such that the stirrup leather is vertical and the heel a little
lower than the toe. Emphasise that you want them to be as

relaxed as possible while keeping in this position. You could mention, particularly, relaxed shoulders, arms and fingers, explaining the movement of a horse's head in walk. Having checked each pupil's position, ask the assistants to lead them round the track again, first on one rein then the other, so you can check both sides.

The horses will probably be plodding lazily round by now, so this is a good opportunity for starting to teach how to produce an active walk. At this stage the assistants can let go of the horses but continue to walk in the same place. Explain the use of the legs. Do *not* ask them to try and squeeze with the legs. Until the riding muscles have developed, and this will not be for several weeks, any attempt at squeezing will only cause the pupil to grip up and probably tighten all the muscles in the body. Gripping up is a very difficult fault to cure and one which should never be allowed to develop. Besides, however advanced a rider becomes, he will from time to time have to get onto a sticky jumper and push it into a fence by using very active lower legs. Now is the time, in the first lessons, to start learning the actual movement involved – taking the lower leg off the horse and putting it on firmly, just behind the girth with the heel still down and no other part of the body moving at the same time. Get the ride to try this action, emphasising that a) they should always try gently first and only increase the strength if they get no response, b) they must make sure that they *allow* the horse to go on and do not stop it by hanging on to the reins and, c) they continue to go with the movement and do not stiffen up.

Having carried out your instructions successfully your pupils should be suitably amazed and gratified at their achievement. At this stage you can explain that what they have done is to use the basic driving aid. Here you could define the term 'aid' because it is a term you will use frequently as they progress. Be careful not to go into too much detail but do explain that the aids become more refined and complicated as a rider becomes more advanced.

This is quite a good time to have the ride brought in and given a lesson in leading, mounting and dismounting. They should be relaxed and receptive and so able to remember what they are told much better than they would have done if you had tried to teach them it right at the beginning. You can use one of your assistants to show how a horse should be led and again for mounting and dismounting. With regard to mounting, make sure you mention that anyone who ever gets on a horse should always check the tightness of the girth before doing anything else, and explain what can happen if they try and mount with a too-loose girth.

I have a bee in my bonnet about mounting, with regard to the rider's left hand. Teach your pupils to put the reins, adjusted to a suitable length to stop the horse moving, in the left hand and also take hold of a large lock of mane, very close to the neck; the right hand pulling them up will be putting a large amount of weight on the saddle and pulling it over to the near side, so do not teach them to mount with their left hand pulling on the saddle as well. There are more than enough equine spinal injuries these days, without taking the risk of causing them in the process of mounting. Tell them to get their weight over the top of the horse as soon as possible. If any of your pupils is very small or not very athletic, get something for him, or her, to stand on. Explain that there is no shame in using a mounting-block and that it is much more important to take care of a horse's back than prove, to those watching, how athletic you are.

Having watched each one mount, you can explain dismounting and get them to try that too. Make sure they realise that one should *spring* off, as well as onto, a horse, not slither.

You can next teach them, in the simplest terms, the transition from an active walk to a halt. Although I have warned against teaching a squeezing action of the lower leg, you must still insist that, when asking for a halt, they close their legs on the horse as well as using the other aids. If you fail to do this, your pupils may get into the habit of asking for a halt with the reins only and that is another bad habit which will he hard to eradicate later.

When they have successfully achieved a halt once or twice, the assistants can come into the middle of the school and the ride can practise walking round the school, halting and walking on again.

In this first lesson you should teach your pupils how to walk round on a completely loose rein, to allow the horse to stretch its neck and the rider to rest. Some people are a little afraid to do this at first, imagining that their horse might run away with them, so apart from resting the horse, walking on a loose rein will build up the pupil's confidence in his horse.

By now the time will probably be up, but the pupils should feel a sense of achievement in the fact that they have learnt to start and stop their horse unaided in their first lesson. It may well be that an hour will prove too long for the first few lessons; if so, do not carry on for the full hour.

Chapter 8

SECOND LESSON

From the start of this lesson begin to ask for correctness of detail. Watch your pupils leading their horses into the school and see whether they have remembered what they were taught in their first lesson. Similarly, when you have checked the tacking up of each horse, watch everyone mount, in turn, and comment on anything they do which is not in accordance with your teaching. Continue to do this meticulously at the beginning of every lesson. This will instil in the pupils' minds the importance of attention to detail.

The second lesson is a good time to teach how to adjust stirrup leathers. One sign of an experienced horseman is his ability to adjust his leathers more by feel than sight, whilst having his horse under control and, if necessary, be able to carry on a conversation at the same time. So tell your pupils that, since they will not always have someone to hold their horse while they use two hands to alter their leathers, they might as well learn how to do it correctly now. If they do, the procedure will soon become second nature to them. For a long time I tried to puzzle out why novice riders, and not only complete novices, almost invariably need two attempts at getting their leathers an equal length. I think I discovered the answer, by watching them carefully; you will find that most of them shift to the right-hand side of the saddle to adjust the left leather and vice versa. The experienced rider, however, will sit squarely in the saddle and merely move his leg from the hip and bend the knee. By doing it that way he is sitting in the same position throughout. So it is a good idea to demonstrate the right and wrong ways, if only to save valuable riding time

. . . . watch your pupils leading their horses in — and see if they have remembered what they were taught . . . .

at the beginning of every lesson. The obvious step from there is an explanation of how to check, and if necessary tighten, the girth before moving off. You should, of course, tell them that they must make a habit of doing this.

Since your ride learnt how to achieve an active walk in their first lesson you should not allow anyone to let his horse wander round the school half asleep. Insist on activity right at the beginning of the lesson. At this stage you will still have your assistants walking beside each horse until everyone has settled down happily. To make sure they have remembered their last lesson, start by correcting bad faults in the basic position and incorrect application of leg. While on the subject of position, always remember that no two people are exactly the same and do not try and insist on a stereotyped position in the saddle. This applies particularly to the feet; some people walk with their toes turned out and some with them turned in and this is bound to affect, to a certain extent, the position in which they put their feet when riding. Also the amount of flexibility in the human ankle varies considerably from person to person and while some can ride easily with their feet in the 'text-book' position, others will have difficulty in getting their heels even slightly lower than their toes.

To return to the lesson, ask the ride to halt and walk on again several times, giving them plenty of warning each time, not asking them to hold the halt too long and timing it so that no horse is going through a corner at the time. As you are about to cover some new ground, ask whether everything is clear so far or if anyone has any questions. Make sure pupils feel that they are free to ask you questions at any suitable time. Relevant questions are better asked when a problem arises than saved until the end of the lesson.

The next thing to teach is steering, but I think before you go into the actual technique, this would be a good time at which to explain the relative unimportance of the reins to beginner riders who have not yet acquired an independent seat. Most people who have had nothing at all to do with horses are quite certain that there is one thing they *do* know — 'You pull on the reins to stop'. It follows, they think, or instinctively feel, that if you do not want the horse to go too fast you keep a firm grip on the reins; when it comes to feeling insecure, they will also instinctively pull on the reins to help keep their balance. It is, after all, instinctive to grab the nearest object if we feel ourselves about to fall. So you must rid your pupils of this idea at an early stage. With docile, well-trained school horses, reins are hardly necessary *if* the horses are kept going forward properly all the time. This is particularly so if you have a more experienced leading file; the other horses will then follow like sheep, even on a loose rein if necessary. Try and instil the idea now that everything starts from the rear-end of the horse, that the motor is at the back and the rider should drive from the back and *allow* the front to go forward. Explain that when they have reached the stage of being able to act quite independently with their hands they will then be expected to keep a light, elastic contact with the horse's mouth, but not until then, or every slight movement of their bodies will be transmitted to the horse's mouth.

You can carry on from here to explain how to turn. Many text-books, when giving the aids for various movements, enumerate them starting from the front of the horse. If you do this your pupils will probably *use* the reins first. Give them the aids *starting with the legs* and explain why you do so. At this stage ask for an open inside rein, but tell them to use as little rein as possible and to try and keep the same rhythm for the walk through the turn. This way they will attach more importance, as they should, to the forward movement than to the change of direction. At this very early stage I think it does more harm than good to ask pupils to use one leg further back than the other or one leg more strongly than the other. They will probably be quite incapable of doing either effectively and while attempting it will, in all probability, forget to keep the horse going forward. You can run through the correct aids for a turn but explain that at this stage all you want them to do is concentrate on keeping the rhythm. Your assistants can continue to walk beside the horses for the moment. Probably the easiest turn to try first will be that required for inclining diagonally across the school and changing the rein. If all goes well the first time, the assistants can come into the centre and let the pupils try it on their own.

In the course of these two lessons you will have had to explain the meaning of such terms as riding 'on the left rein' and so on; explain each term as it is needed — 'inside rein', 'outside rein', 'leading file', 'incline diagonally' etc. While on this subject, I think there are two good reasons for using the terms 'inside' and 'outside' (leg and rein) as far as possible, instead of 'left' and 'right'. Firstly, there are a few people, adults as well as children, who have genuine difficulty in sorting out their left from their right. Secondly, using the terms 'inside' and 'outside' from the beginning will encourage right thinking with regard to the bending of the horse, with which they will be concerned later on. You will, of course, have to make use of 'left' and 'right' when asking for turns. If you should have a pupil who really cannot remember which is which, you can always suggest he emulates the lady of whom I once heard, who drew a large capital 'L' on the back of her left hand and a large capital 'R' on the back of her right hand, before having a driving lesson!

If the whole ride is able to change direction while continuing to go forward properly, you can then ask them to turn across the school in single file at the half-markers or down the centre from the middle of the short sides. Both these turns require stronger leg and more tactful use of the reins if the forward movement is to be maintained. You will probably find that when they first start to turn down the centre or across the school at the half-markers, that they will not start the turn until they actually reach the markers and consequently have to loop back to the centre line. It will be necessary to explain that they must so time the turn that they do not go *over* the centre line. It is a good idea to give everyone a turn as leading file for these turns as the leading file naturally has the most difficult task. If this is all carried out satisfactorily they can then try turning left or right simultaneously across the school, instead of in single file.

In this lesson, so long as everyone is confident, they can be asked to ride for a few minutes without stirrups and it is a good idea to teach them a few exercises at the halt to finish with. Exercises have two purposes – to develop balance and grip and to eliminate stiffness. If the pupils are only able to have a lesson once a week, exercises as a means of developing balance and grip will probably not achieve very much, but they are always of value, whatever the frequency of lessons, as a means of eliminating stiffness. Children seem to enjoy them particularly and they are a means of making a children's ride seem more of a game than a lesson.

Chapter 9

THIRD LESSON

I have been assuming that the three pupils are average sort of adults and suggested a suitably average sort of program for such people. However, if your pupils should happen to be particularly athletic, show no signs of nervousness and appear to find everything fairly easy, then obviously you will be able to cover more ground in a shorter time. As a general rule though, remember that the rate of progress cannot, to any great extent, exceed the rate of development of the riding muscles. Some people may be quite ready to start trotting in the second lesson and some can manage quite happily without being led almost from the start; whether or not this is possible will, of course, also depend on the type of horses you are using. So do not be hidebound and stick to a rigid formula, regardless.

To return to our three average, not particularly athletic, adult beginners who are about to start their third lesson, start by doing your usual checks of mounting, adjusting girths and stirrup leathers, etc., then tell them in what order you want them to ride round. It should not be necessary for anyone to be led at the beginning. At this stage it is quite a good idea to explain, as they are walking round, that a horse should always be warmed up when it is brought out of the stable, to avoid muscular strain. Explain that even when, much later on, they are capable of cantering and jumping, they must never ask either of these things of a horse until it has been properly ridden in at the walk and trot.

After five or ten minutes you should ask your pupils whether they are quite sure their stirrups feel right. At this stage it will still be necessary, sometimes, to say that *you* think a particular person is riding too long or too short, as the case may be, because they are not sufficiently experienced to know for certain themselves. If someone does need to alter his stirrups, tell him to put the reins in one hand and keep his horse walking round while he makes the adjustment; the sooner they all become capable of doing this, the better. Remember that a lesson with stirrups uneven or the wrong length is a wasted lesson. Having made sure that everyone is comfortable, ask the ride to do some turns and see that the last lesson has been remembered properly. It is always a good idea to start by revising the previous lessons, especially in the early stages.

If you have not, so far, had an experienced person as leading file, you will need one now; at least, it will be much easier if you do have. If this proves impossible, it will be necessary to borrow someone's horse. Ask the ride to turn in up one end of the school and halt, off the track, while you explain all about the trot. Ask your experienced rider to trot round at a slow, steady pace so that the pupils can see the horse's diagonal legs moving as a pair. Incidentally, a grey horse or one with white legs is much better for this than a dark-coloured one, indoors. Tell them about the two different ways to ride at the trot and ask your demonstrator to show them first riding then sitting while you talk about them. Although at first they will not have to do it, it is also worth explaining that, as soon as they are able, they will learn to rise and sit on either diagonal and tell them why this is necessary.

You will now need an assistant to lead each horse; tell the pupils that at first you want them to leave the control of the horse entirely to the leader and just get the feel of the trot. They should make sure they have no contact with the horse's mouth and take the neck strap as well as the reins in both hands. At first ask for a sitting trot and tell them to try and keep the correct position and absorb the movement of the horse by staying relaxed, particularly in their hips and knees. The leaders should try to ensure that the horses trot as slowly as possible and short spells of this should be interrupted for short rests at the walk. A few people seem to imagine that as soon as their horse trots for the first time they are bound to fall off, so this initial period of trotting also serves the purpose of disproving this idea. After a few minutes, stop the ride trotting; it is very tiring for novice riders and also for horses with novice riders on their backs.

Halt your ride — there is no need to bring them off the track this time — and explain how they should try and rise to the trot. Having tried all sorts of dodges for helping people achieve this, I have come to the conclusion that there are really only two things which help. First, impress on them that their up and down movement must be continuous; this sounds too obvious to mention but it is surprising how many people get themselves up out of the saddle very nicely and then seem to hang in mid-air, if this point is not made. Since I tried the second thing, I have had any number of what I call 'first-timers' — pupils managing to get the correct rhythm at the very first attempt — whereas, prior to using this method, I could count the 'first-timers' on the fingers of one hand. Go up to each pupil in turn, ask him to drop the reins, fold his arms and raise himself up over the pommel, by inclining the shoulders forward and pushing up from the feet. Tell him you want him to stay up for a moment and then lower himself slowly into the saddle. At first he will keep falling back into the saddle and his legs will swing forward but after several attempts he will manage to balance himself, with his feet directly underneath him. Then tell him, that is what a rising trot is — doing that continuously, in time with the horse's movement. When

. . . . *to stop this one crouching like a monkey* . . . .

you have seen everyone do this, tell the whole ride to pick up their reins, still with no contact, and also their neck straps, and get them to walk on, with the assistants leading, of course.

The pupils, by stronger use of their legs than they have previously had to use, should be able to get their horses into a trot and the assistants should be able to keep them going at a steady pace. The pace should be more brisk than for the sitting trot or the movement of the horse will not help sufficiently with the pupils' rising. Each assistant can now help his own rider by counting '1', '2', or 'up', 'down', at the speed the pupil should be rising, while you watch from the centre of the school. Do not ask them to trot for more than a few moments without returning to a walk, so they can rest. Everyone puts far too much effort into these early attempts at rising and no good can come of continuing to try with aching muscles, out of which all elasticity has temporarily gone. Impress on them that the action should *not* be tiring and that it will not be, when they are used to it. Explain that little more is necessary than to incline the upper part of the body forward whilst pushing down into the heel and that the horse will do the rest. Tell them also that they should try not to rise higher out of the saddle than necessary.

At this stage do not correct position; the only thing of any importance is that they should learn to feel the rhythm and rise in time to the trot. Once that is established you can begin to stop this one crouching like a monkey and that one sticking his legs forward and pulling himself up on the neck strap.

Again, if time allows, finish the lesson with a few exercises at the halt. In the very early stages, exercises help to make the pupils feels at home on a horse and to this end it is alright to save them until the last part of the lesson, but if the prime object is to overcome stiffness, it is better to do the exercises early on in the lesson.

Chapter 10

FOURTH LESSON

In this lesson, as soon as everyone is comfortable and you have spent a short time with the ride in walk, have them trotting. The sooner everyone has achieved a rising trot, the sooner the whole ride will be able to start making real progress. If anyone has great difficulty in rising, tell him to try rising only two or three times before he sits for a few steps and then tries rising again; this way, his muscles will be rested slightly between each attempt.

These periods of trotting, since they are very tiring at first, should be interspersed with periods of work at the walk. As the pupils should now feel secure at the walk, you can come to the subject of trying to keep a nice elastic contact with the horse's mouth, in walk. Explain that by keeping contact with the mouth, through the reins, and having the legs close to the horse's sides, a rider is in constant communication with his horse; the horse will thus be attentive and ready to answer to the aids for changes of pace and direction when they are given. Bring your assistants into the centre and let your ride try keeping contact, while doing frequent turns and changes of rein.

Having spent a short time at this, remembering to check faults in position, get the ride trotting again. Those who are able to pick up the rhythm every time should not need to be led any more and should be able to give some of their attention to keeping their horse going and to steering. Obviously they will not, yet, be completely independant of the reins, so tell them to adjust their reins in both hands so they are short enough for control, take the neck strap as well, in the inside hand, and keep the outside hand free to use the outside rein. They should thus be able to keep their horse out on the track – unless it happens to be one of those unco-operative creatures which likes to go into a corner and stop.

As soon as your pupils are capable of trotting round the school and can sustain a rising trot for a reasonable period, start to correct faults in position. Do not do so before this, unless it is quite obvious that it is a faulty position which is causing the difficulty in rising to the trot; if you do, they will have too many different things to think about. It is not always easy, but try not to ask anyone to work at more than one fault at a time.

Whilst on the subject of faults, try and work out the reason for them, rather than merely telling the pupils what he is doing incorrectly; for example, 'You can't get yourself out of the saddle because your legs have gone forward and you are behind the movement.' If someone has a very bad fault such as leaning forward with rounded shoulders, it is sometimes necessary to tell him to sit up and lean *back*. A renowned teacher once said, 'When straightening a crooked stick it will be necessary to bend it more in the other direction before it is made straight.' If you have to exaggerate someone's position in this way, it is a good idea to explain to everyone why you are going it, or someone, who only heard you with half his attention, may go away thinking one should lean back when riding; what is more, he may quote you as having said so.

Another movement you can teach in a break from the trotting is trying to ride a large circle at the walk. As with the changes of rein, give everyone a turn as leading file, since this is the most demanding position in which to be. It is surprising how very difficult most people find riding a circle at first. Before they start, emphasise that they must look up and look ahead to where they want to go, as they would when driving a car or riding a bicycle. Again, impress on them that if they keep their horses going forward actively all the time, they should have no difficulty. It is when they forget to drive that the horses will decide that the shortest way back to the track is a straight line. You can explain the correct aids for riding on a circle but make sure that they do not, in consequence, attach more importance to where to use inside and outside leg than to forward movement. This is also quite a good time to tell them that they should begin to use a less open inside rein but to be careful not to put backward tension on it.

It is not too early for a short spell of work without stirrups at the walk and also some of the more simple exercises at the walk. Be sure to explain that none of the exercises is of any value if the pupil allows himself to lose position when carrying them out.

At some stage when a rest seems indicated, probably after another spell of trotting, it is useful to ask them to try riding individually. Line the ride up in the centre of the school and ask each person to walk out onto the track and round the school, on his own. If he has not previously appreciated that it is necessary to drive his horse on continually, rather than sit on it and let it follow the one in front, he will now. Here you want horses with minds of their own, which will re-join the other horses unless kept going forward properly. This is a time when the riders who have difficulty will probably go rigid in every muscle and bang away with both legs to no avail. Impress on everyone that the legs must be independent and while they are being used, the upper part of the body must stay relaxed and go with the movement of the horse. If this does prove to be a difficult exercise, do not ask for more than one complete circuit of the school, but make sure that when it is finished, they *ride* their horses back into their places in the middle, instead of allowing them to merely re-join the others.

Chapter 11

FIFTH LESSON

We have come to the fifth lesson and I have not, so far, mentioned whips or sticks. Beginners should start to carry one as soon as possible, certainly as soon as they are no longer led. Often, they say they would prefer not to, because they get it muddled up with the reins, but insist that they do carry one; learning to carry it correctly is as important as learning to hold the reins correctly. It may be that in the very early stages they will not actually use it, but that is not a good reason for not learning to carry it and, particularly, learning to change it, in the correct manner, from one hand to the other. By this lesson, they should have some idea of how to use a whip. Beginners are very prone to giving an ineffective tap on the horse's shoulder, without taking their hand off the reins. Teach them the correct way of putting the reins into one hand and using the stick behind their leg. Come down heavily on anyone who uses it on the shoulder in the way mentioned above. Tell them that if they keep their hand on the reins when applying the whip, they are almost bound to 'job' the horse in the mouth. Remind them also that with a lazy horse, the whip is used to reinforce the leg aid and so it *must* be used just behind the leg. Of course, long schooling whips should never be used by anyone until they have acquired an independent seat.

We will assume that, by the start of this fifth lesson, everyone has mastered the rising trot, even if their position in the saddle when performing it still leaves much to be desired. Those who are able to go well with the horse and not get left behind, can now take their reins normally in both hands and dispense with the neck strap. However, this is a good time to remind them that if they seem to be losing their balance at any time, they must never clutch at the reins for support but grab the mane or neck strap. If any of your pupils is in any doubt about his ability to rise to the trot without something to hold on to, get the whole ride to knot their reins on the horse's necks; they should then trot on, holding the knot at first and, once the trot is established, leave go of the knot and continue trotting with their hands in the normal riding position. By having the reins knotted, they are in a position to regain control very quickly if their horses should decide to go too fast or in the wrong direction. This is a good exercise and helps to improve balance and build up confidence.

It will still be necessary to be careful not to tire your pupils by asking them to trot for too long at a time, so have them working in walk frequently. By this time you should have started to be firm about distances between horses. Discourage sloppy riding and try and encourage them to keep about one horse's length behind the horse in front without your having to be continually asking them to close up or spread out. Teach them to cut a corner deliberately, in order to close a gap, rather than increase their speed and destroy the rhythm. Make it clear that this insistance on correct distances has no militaristic overtones. Explain that when they are correctly spaced, you can see them better, they can hear you better and that even this business of keeping their distance is a test of accurate riding and is good practice in control.

At this stage they should be ready for short spells of slow trotting without stirrups. This will help to get them relaxed and develop a deep seat. If someone seems to have particularly poor balance and obviously will gain nothing from being asked to do this, let him take up his stirrups again. But provided they have their horses going in a slow, 'lazy' trot, there should be no difficulty and they can revert to having one hand on the neck strap if they feel the need. During the walking part of their work without stirrups, get them to do some exercises.

This will be a good time for your ride to make their first serious attempt at a sitting trot *with* stirrups, so try this for a short period, remembering that it is very tiring for both rider and horse. I think having had some practice at sitting to the trot helps when it comes to early cantering. Although the movement is not the same at the trot and canter, it is necessary, at both paces, to relax and absorb the movement with the hips and knees. It helps to get used to doing so first at a slow trot when there is little or no risk of losing the balance.

After a rest and some more work in walk, ask them to trot on in succession and take the rear. Control will probably still be rather poor but do insist that the corners are not cut. You will have explained, before, how they should keep their horse trotting by using their legs each time their seat comes into the saddle, so this will be a chance to see if they are able to do so effectively. Be careful to check that they do not let their legs swing when they do this. At this stage they will no doubt use the rear file as a buffer and do little, themselves, towards asking the horse to walk when they come up to the back of the ride. This is acceptable at their first attempt, but tell them that in their next lesson you will be dealing with downward transitions and then they will learn how to do this properly.

Chapter 12

SIXTH LESSON

In any group of pupils there may be one or two who are late starters, in the sense that the lesson is half over before they really seem to achieve anything. In some cases this is due to nervousness, so obviously you must try and build up such people's confidence and get them relaxed as soon as possible; if they are stiff their horse will not go properly for them anyway, so it is a vicious circle. If the reason is merely a passive sort of approach to riding, then probably the best results will be obtained by driving these people a little harder than the others at the beginning of the lesson. Riding school horses do, of course, become very skilled at summing up the ability of their riders and if they decide that, with this particular one, there is no need to work, then the rider will probably have a difficult time. Explain this and try and encourage everyone to be business-like in their attitude from the word 'go'. Tell them to expect obedience and activity from their horse as soon as they move off after mounting. If your ride is trailing round looking like a funeral procession, tell them so, and if they do not get the required result by using their legs, remind them that they have whips, and make sure that they use them properly. Many novices think it is cruel to hit a horse, so explain that if they use the whip quite firmly *at the moment of disobedience*, they will probably not have to do it again, as the horse will respect them. Tell them also that it is much more unkind to thump a horse in the ribs continuously for a solid hour and that if they do, they will eventually deaden the horse's sides and get even less response.

As soon as you have your riders and horses warmed up, give

them a period without stirrups at walk and trot and a few exercises at the walk. I think that novices, especially, benefit by having the work without stirrups, as well as the exercises, early in the lesson, because it relaxes them and gets them down into the saddle and they will then progress more quickly once they have taken up their stirrups again.

Your ride should now have reached the stage of being able to change rein at the trot without loss of rhythm. Start them doing this by inclining diagonally across the school and changing the rein and ask for a stronger use of the inside leg on the turns and round the corners of the school. When they manage this fairly efficiently they can try changing rein at the half markers, but the right-angled turn involved in this may prove too difficult at first. If you find they are forgetting to give the horse warning of the impending turn and are tending to haul it round on the reins, then leave this movement for a later lesson. It is widely taught that in any movement involving coming off the track in trot, the rider should change from a rising to a sitting trot, but it is better for novice riders to continue rising, or their horses are very likely to lose the rhythm as they change direction. Besides, novice riders will not be working in a sitting trot at all in the early stages, so it is better to introduce the custom later, if you wish to introduce it.

Now for the transition from trot to walk. If, from the start, you lay great stress on the fact that this is a *forward* movement, with the drive coming from behind, you may be able to educate your pupils so that later, they will instinctively bring the horse's hocks under him when decreasing speed. Teach these transitions in such a way that your pupils will not, in the future, regard the driving aids involved as a refinement of dressage and totally unnecessary in the hunting field, for example. Remind them that the motor is at the back, that the horse should be balanced and that they cannot achieve this state of balance by acting only on the front of the horse. Also remind them that the action of the legs and seat must always, if only fractionally, precede the action of the hands.

The easiest way for them to try the transition from trot to walk is probably to trot in succession to the rear of the ride. This way, they will receive some help from their horse, which will want to stop anyway. It is a good thing to allow it to be a fairly lengthy process at first, so let them, from rising, sit to the trot, slow the pace and then apply the aids a little more strongly to ask for walk. When they have all tried this two or three times you will want to check whether they are being effective with their aids. One of the best ways of doing this is to ask them to go from trot to walk when they have only reached the half-way point on the way round to the rear of the ride. Tell each pupil at what point you want him to walk and suggest the place where he should start to give the aids for the transition. Be careful to time this so that his horse is not at such a place that it sees the rest of the horses straight in front of it, or it may not wish to slow down.

By this sixth lesson some of your pupils, if not all, may feel they would like to try a canter. Ideally, from the point of view of security and progress, this is better left much longer, but it is a matter of what the pupil wants and retaining interest. If someone says he does not feel ready, then do not press him, he will be able to learn quite a lot from watching the others, anyway. To try and force a pupil to canter for the first time achieves nothing, because he will probably be so stiff and tensed-up that it can only prove to be an uncomfortable experience; and there is also a chance that someone so apprehensive may fall off.

Strictly speaking, the easiest place to canter for the first time is out of doors, on a slightly up-hill slope, but this is only safe on a horse that can be completely relied on to stop at the top. There is no doubt that cantering round the corners of an indoor school or manège can unseat beginners, so only ask them to canter on the straight, at first.

There are two schools of thought about beginners going into a canter; some people maintain that it is easier from a walk and others from a trot. There are points in favour of both. If the horse will go smoothly from a walk, then this must be the easiest for a beginner, because he will not have time to lose his position in the saddle, nor be so likely to, while applying the aids. If, on the other hand, the horses are not sufficiently well-schooled to do this, then trot to canter is the only way.

To return to our three pupils, we will assume that they would all like to canter and that they have horses which are not schooled in walk to canter, since this is the case with most riding school horses. Bring them into the middle of the school and tell them something about the pace. If you have an experienced rider present (if not, it will have to be you), ask him to demonstrate the canter to them so that they can watch the horse's legs and note the leading ones. Explain the aids for asking a horse to canter on a named leg but make it clear to the ride that you will not want them to try and give these aids until they are quite secure and comfortable in the canter. Then draw attention to how your demonstrator sits to the canter. You can prove how essential relaxation is by asking this rider to stiffen his back and knees and then point out how he bounces in the saddle.

I think one of the reasons a previously relaxed and confident pupil tends to become frightened in his first canter is because he ceases to feel in control of the situation; this is probably because the increased speed makes it seem as if everything is happening too fast. (Remember that we are dealing with typical riding school horses — I am not suggesting that the canter had always to be faster than the trot). I have found that one can avoid alarming pupils if they can be persuaded to think of their early cantering as merely trotting in succession to the rear of the ride, and cantering a few strides on the way round. Tell your ride that you will talk each of them through the exercise and to try and listen carefully and do exactly as you tell them. Impress on them that you want them to have their horses fully under control all the time and there is to be no severe corner cutting. Tell them that you will want an active trot and that they must drive the horse on quite strongly but not allow it to increase its speed. Say that when each person comes to the last corner before he comes up to the rear of the ride, you will tell him to sit to the trot, take the neck strap with his inside hand only, use both legs strongly and lighten his contact with the horse's mouth to *allow* it to go into canter. Emphasise that you want only a few strides of canter before he does a downward transition to trot, commences rising and trots on to take rear file. When you actually take each rider through this you should be fairly close to his horse — approximately where you would stand if lunging the horse — and then you can help the pupil into canter by the use of your voice, as you would if the horse was on the lunge. So long as the pupil remembers to lighten, or even drop, the contact at the right moment, the horse should canter on without any trouble.

All the above may seem unnecessarily detailed and fussy but I have seen too many inexperienced instructors not taking sufficient care, with the result that at their first attempt at a canter, a pupil falls off. If a beginner is not helped sufficiently he will stiffen up as soon as his horse breaks into a canter, forget to steer and be carried, probably by means of a tight circle, back to the other horses. It is when the horse is turning sharply that he may fall off. By the method I have outlined the pupil *does* feel in control and the number of cantering strides can be gradually increased as his confidence grows, until he can manage to carry on right round the school. Very early on it will be necessary to teach your pupils to use their legs lightly at every stride. Apart from the necessity of this, with most horses, to keep them in canter, using the legs helps to keep the rider in position. There is another, not unimportant, reason for wanting the pupil to be in control of the horse, even in his first canter; the more school horses are allowed to have their own way, the more difficult they become for beginners to ride. It is true, it is not desirable to get a horse into such a state that it will never attempt to assert its own will, but when it comes to pupils' early cantering efforts, it is much better for the horses to learn that, even if they can get away with trotting when they are supposed to be cantering, on *no* account will they be allowed to steer their own course back to the other horses.

As I said earlier, most people are not strictly ready to canter as soon as this and only a little time should be spent on it in the early lessons. However, to have cantered does give a pupil a great sense of achievement and he will feel he has really started to get somewhere.

Chapter 13

MAINLY ABOUT SAFETY

Given average progress and reliable horses, pupils who have had half a dozen lessons in an enclosed space, should be ready to venture out on a quiet hack. After all the concentrated hard work they will have done in their previous lessons, a ride out will be relaxing and enjoyable and they will be able to put into practice all they have learnt inside. Make this first hack a very leisurely affair — walk fast, trot slowly and do not canter at all. Take a couple of leading reins with you, just in case the need for them arises and make sure you are riding a sensible horse yourself, so that you can give nearly all your attention to your pupils.

It is a good thing for beginners to continue to ride out periodically, say between every four or five lessons. If you have not already done so, explain that lessons are given in a school or manège for safety and to aid concentration and ease of instructing. Point out that many horses well within the scope of beginners inside, will be well beyond their capabilities outside. Explain that indoor riding is a means to an end, and not an end in itself. If the basics which have been drummed into them inside are applied when riding outside, they should have no difficulty in controlling an average, well-mannered horse.

Some people who have learnt most of their riding in an indoor school tend to become over confident, in the sense that they know they can walk, trot, canter and perhaps jump 3 feet, and unless enlightened by an instructor, have reason to suppose that they are ready to ride an unknown horse in the open. It may be that they know someone who has a horse wasting in a field, because its owner has no time to ride it and has offered to let them do so. This pupil may not realise that a horse that has not be ridden for some months may be over-full of itself when it is first taken out. He may never have ridden a horse which shies violently, is nappy or bucks lightheartedly when put into a canter. The result may be a nasty fall and certainly disillusionment, if no broken bones.

So take every opportunity you can of teaching your pupils the basics, not only of good riding but also of self-preservation when on a horse. The instinctive reaction of a novice rider to trouble, such as shying, his horse trying to kick another horse, or taking too strong a hold, almost invariably seems to be to snatch at the reins, draw up the heels and freeze. Talk to your pupils about this and try and train them to push down into the heel and grip with the knees when an emergency arises. Explain also that if a horse is made to go forward, he will be unable to do much else; for example, if a horse tries to kick another one, push it on vigourously. Tell them that if they ride their horses properly on the bit when out hacking, as in the school, few troubles are likely to occur. In the early days, more often than not, most troubles do seem to stem from the fact that most riding school horses are, in the main, quite content to plod along, rather like a herd of elephants, following the one in front of them and their novice riders sit passively on top allowing them to do this; so remind them to *ride* their horses and remain in control.

Training can be given, after fifteen lessons or so, in trying to prevent a pupil getting into a state of panic if a horse 'takes off' with him. Get him to think coolly and calmly about such an eventuality. Point out that if he instinctively draws up his heels, possibly even grips the horse with his heels, and goes rigid with fear, he will probably fall off in no time.

Have your ride standing in a group in a field and give them

. . . . to plod along, rather like a herd of elephants . . . .

a demonstration of pulling up from high speed. Canter round them fast, on a large circle, and then, with half halts, slow down and finally halt your horse smoothly in as short a distance as possible. Then get each pupil to canter round on a large circle, but not too fast. (Incidentally before your pupils canter out on a hack, you should teach them the position to adopt for a fast canter or a gallop because, in the main, horses tend to canter faster out of doors than in the school if they have the passenger-type of pupil on board, and your pupils may be bounced off if they try and stay down in the saddle). When your circling pupil has got going nicely, say you want him to imagine he is being run away with and try and pull up, not roughly, but as quickly as possible; this way you can check each rider's position and see whether he keeps his heels down, sits deep and uses his back and legs to slow down his horse. When everyone has tried this, tell them that if ever a horse starts to go too fast, they must not panic, simply do as they have just done. Also tell them that if they find a horse is too strong for them and they have the space, they should try turning in a large circle and keep the horse going round until it wants to stop. You can show them how, with an over-strong horse, you can wedge one hand firmly on the mane and work on the rein on the other side. Explain that a dead pull on both reins is almost certain to make any horse go faster.

Finally remind them that in certain rare circumstances there can come a time when the safest thing to do is get off. You do not want to foster an idea of 'when in doubt, bale out', but if an un-stopable horse is galloping straight for a deep railway cutting, that is the time to decide that a human life is more important than a horse's.

Do not give such a safety lesson too early in your pupil's riding career. When you do, try to do it in such a way that you will not build up fear in previously happy and confident pupils. Do not be an alarmist, only rather matter-of-fact, and impress on them that such circumstances may never arise in their experience.

In general try to see that falls are kept to a minimum; they rarely benefit anyone and it is only too easy for a novice rider to have a fall which causes him to lose his nerve. If a pupil does fall off, try and discover why it happened so that you can do your best to prevent a repetition. If he merely lost his balance, it may be that you are pushing him too fast. If the horse ducked back to the others in the middle of the school after a jump, when going on the left rein, remind the pupil that as he comes up to the jump next time he must use his left leg and right rein on landing, and so on. There are some people who have never fallen off, whose terror of falls, in itself, retards their general progress hopelessly; to such people, a painless fall on soft ground *can* be beneficial. They realise that a fall can be quite harmless and from then on, relax and make progress. However, no one would recommend attempting to engineer a fall for this purpose; there would be far too much risk attached. You can tell your pupils that if they do reach the point of no return, they should try and let themselves go, refrain from putting out a hand to try and break their fall and to try and roll as they land. You can *tell* them, but until they become fairly experienced at falling off, they will probably automatically try and resist and go rigid.

When you take your pupils out hacking teach them how to ride on roads. Also try and teach them, in a not too obvious way, a certain amount of country lore and the generally accepted behaviour when riding across country. Your pupils may be town-dwellers who know nothing about not riding over crops, for example. You can make sure they all learn how to open and shut gates by seeing to it that everyone has a turn at doing so.

Chapter 14

THE SEVENTH AND SUCCEEDING LESSONS

This is not too early to introduce a few trotting poles and a lesson in the jumping position, but do not spend too long on it in the early stages, rather work at improving balance and control and developing riding muscles. Start to ask for more precision in general, but only very slowly. Try to get your pupils to 'think' a movement before, and while, applying the aids for it, and begin to ask for more accurate aids. Whilst on the subject of the aids, try not to produce riders who have a 'text-book' approach to them; in other words, when they wish, for example, to ride a circle, they merely apply the aids as laid down in the books, regardless of what is going on underneath them at that moment. If you have put it over in the right way, your pupil, eventually (though not by his seventh lesson), should think — have I enough impulsion, is my horse going forward properly, is he swinging his quarters out, is he falling in to the circle? — and act accordingly. But of course he should be feeling rather than thinking.

Try to develop 'feel' in your pupils and encourage them to look on the aids as a language which will be understood by the horse if the words are pronounced clearly and correctly.

Perhaps the most difficult people to teach are those who come to you when they have been riding for a year or two, have been badly taught, or not taught at all, but have read all the books they could find. Because they have ridden for a relatively long time and are secure on a horse, they seem totally unable to see that they ride badly, do not understand the basic essentials and have no 'feel'. Because they know the aids for all the movements, in theory, they do not understand why, if they do as the books say, they cannot produce a smooth rein-back or shoulder-in, or whatever the movement is. I might have been thinking of such pupils when I mentioned the need for tact in an instructor because this is one type of pupil with whom you will need all the tact you can muster.

But I am digressing. To return to the second half-dozen lessons and thereafter, you may have found that each pupil has one particular difficulty and it will be necessary to try and think out solutions to these difficulties. One of the most common is learning to sit to the canter. If you have a pupil who seems perfectly secure, it will help initially if he canters without stirrups as often as possible. He should soon find he stops bouncing and remains in the saddle this way. There can, however, be one rather tiresome side-effect of this treatment; he may tend to grip up to retain his balance at first and when he again canters with stirrups, he will probably have difficulty keeping suficient weight in them to retain them. But this difficulty should be easier to overcome than the bouncing. If being unable to sit to the canter is caused by nervousness, the above treatment would do more harm than good. If you feel confident that this pupil has not, in fact, been asked to canter too early, you may well find his problem is best dealt with by including him in the early jumping lessons. If he trots round the school, then, a stride or two away from the pole, sits down and pushes his horse on vigorously, in all probability it will land in canter and continue in canter for a few strides. You need not even comment on the fact that he is cantering. It is sometimes surprising how, when he is busy pushing the horse on over the jump and keeping it straight afterwards, he seems to fail to notice he is cantering. If this practice is continued for a while, his confidence may suddenly come.

As soon as your pupils are reasonably secure and sitting

fairly well in canter, in fact as soon as they reach the stage of being able to think of other things besides staying on and not bouncing in the saddle, you should start to ask more of them. Every time his horse canters ask each pupil which leads it is on. If he cannot tell you, ask the rest of the ride. The sooner they all start having to think about this, the sooner they will learn to feel whether they are right or wrong. Work at the build-up of impulsion and a smooth transition from trot to canter and although you will still only ask for the transition in a corner, the pupils should now be trying to apply the aids for canter correctly. You can begin to ask for a good downward transition, too, instead of the horses being allowed to sprawl into a trot. When they have progressed along these lines, ask them sometimes to canter *past* the ride and take the rear the second time round. This is usually fairly difficult for the novice, who does not, at first, realise how hard he must work to get his horse past the others; similarly if he is asked to canter a circle on his way round the school, which is another good exercise.

Your ride can attempt half halts quite early. They may not execute them very well but they encourage right thinking, i.e., from the back to the front of the horse and discourage the practice of giving a dead pull on both reins. When they are more advanced, a good way of finding out how effective their half halts are, is to ask them to slow the canter, when on their way round to the rear of the ride, and then increase the pace again. If they are not using their back, seat and legs correctly, their horse will probably break into a trot.

As soon as their rising trot is easy and relaxed and their riding in general is fairly smooth, teach rising on either diagonal. A sign of having introduced this too early, will be if you see your pupils forgetting everything else in an attempt to find out on which diagonal they are rising and sitting. If this does occur, it is best to tell them to forget about it for the time being; you can bring it in again later. Assuming it is *not* too early, begin by explaining that if a rider always rises and sits on one diagonal, a horse becomes stiff on the other. There is no need to go more deeply into the matter than that at this stage. Do not say that there is a *correct* diagonal on which to rise and sit, rather that, in this country, it is generally accepted that it is best to ride on the outside diagonal, i.e., when riding on the left rein, the rider rises as the off fore and near hind legs go forward and sits when these legs are on the ground and vice-versa on the right rein.

This is a somewhat complicated subject to teach. I think the best way to start, having introduced it in the way suggested above, is to ask an experienced rider to trot on, let us say, a large left-handed circle up one end of the school. Most people seem to find it easier to learn to judge which diagonal they are on by using the 'rise' rather than the 'sit' part of the movement, in conjunction with the action of the horse's legs. As your demonstrator rises, say 'up-down' in time to his movement and tell your pupils to watch the horse's forelegs, explaining that on the word 'up', the off foreleg will go forward.

The next thing to explain is changing from one diagonal to the other, emphasising that if it is too difficult, at first, to change by sitting for only one 'bump', they must sit for three — at least, never for an even number, or they will end up on the same diagonal as before. When your demonstrator shows how this is done, make sure he is broadside on to the ride at the time. A demonstration of changing diagonals is not, perhaps, of very much value at this stage, as this action can really only be learned by 'feel' on the part of each individual. You will find that pupils will learn to know which diagonal they are on, and to change from one to the other, much more quickly than they will acquire the ability to judge which diagonal *another* rider is on.

Having completed the explanation and demonstration, have the ride trotting round the school on the right rein. Tell them to say to themselves (silently), 'up — down' as they rise and sit, then to glance down at their horse's shoulders to see which one goes forward on the word 'up'. When they have tried this for a few minutes, ask each pupil in turn which diagonal he thinks he is on. With some, it may be necessary to say 'up — down' for them, while they watch the point of the shoulder.

The reason for starting this exercise on the right rein is because most riding school horses will be more comfortable to ride that way and, consequently, the pupils will find it easier to rise on the left diagonal. However, *because* of this and the fact that their consequent success may have been more a matter of good luck than judgment, you should then get them to practise the same exercise on the other rein.

As soon as everyone is able to tell you correctly nearly every time, which diagonal he is on, proceed to the change. At this stage, do not ask for a change of rein as well, as this will make everything even more complicated. Tell everyone to try changing from one diagonal to the other and back again. Give them a few minutes to practise before you make any comment, then deal with each pupil separately. Ask which diagonal he thinks he is on, tell him to change, and then ask again which he is on. Give them all plenty of time to answer as it is a very confusing matter for a novice.

Do not spend too long on the subject of diagonals the first time, and make sure you do not end a lesson with it, but return to the subject in every lesson thereafter until everyone feels confident. Once they do, make it clear that in future you will expect them all to rise and sit on the outside diagonal at all times. This will be brought home to everyone if, as soon as the ride trots in any lesson, you correct anyone who happens to be on the inside diagonal.

Remember to point out, when you first introduce the subject, that when hacking, hunting or exercising, one should change the diagonals periodically, even though one is apparently riding on the straight. If this is not emphasised, your pupils may regard it as something which it is only necessary to bother about when riding in a confined space.

As an alternative to the periodic hack, in times of bad weather for example, you could introduce mounted games. Apart from being enjoyable and a pleasant break from hard work, they are beneficial in themselves. You must, however, make sure that enthusiasm and a keen competitive spirit does not cause anyone to forget all the good training you have given them and resort to rough methods of riding. These games need not require a large number of 'props'. You can, for example, use buckets as bending poles. If you are unable to procure potatoes, perhaps there will be carrots in the feed-room which you can borrow for a potato race. The carrots can be put in a pile on top of an oil-drum up one end of the school and carried, one by one, up to the other end to be dropped into a bucket, although of course there is a risk of the horses getting to the carrots before their riders. Another alternative is a tacking up race, if your pupils can do this. In fact you will probably be able to think of many other games besides those mentioned, but do not have any which involve riding at high speed, as these might prove dangerous.

You can vary ordinary lessons by teaching vaulting on, mounting and dis-mounting on the off-side and dismounting when in motion.

Ask questions during your lessons, not only to see if your pupils remember what they are taught but sometimes to see what ideas they have about something that has not yet been

. . . . a risk of the horses getting to the carrots before their riders . . . .

. . . . prevent these occasions turning into an excuse for idle chatter . . . .

covered. When a pupil asks you a question, if you think one of the others may be able to answer it, give him the chance; you can always enlarge on his reply if it is inadequate, or correct it if it is wrong. Do anything you can to turn your pupils into thinking riders, if they are not naturally so, and to encourage their interest in riding as an art.

When pupils are performing an exercise individually, especially if the rest of the ride is gathered in the middle of the school, try to draw these others in, by telling them that you will ask for their comments afterwards. This is a good practice for two reasons, firstly, everyone can learn by watching other people and developing their critical faculty and secondly, it will prevent these occasions turning into an excuse for idle chatter among the rest of the ride. When each person is riding individually like this, let him try whatever movement or exercise you have asked for, without helping him or trying to talk him through it the first time. If, after discussing with him and the rest of the ride what went right and what went wrong, you want him to try it again, then this time give him any help he needs. By talking someone through a movement, in other words, riding his horse in your imagination, and telling him when to apply one leg or the other, and so on, you will develop 'feel' in him.

Chapter 15

JUMPING LESSONS

I believe in starting jumping lessons early. So many people nowadays, adults in particular, come to riding thinking, 'I want to learn to ride but I don't think I want to learn to jump', as if these were two quite separate activities. If you introduce it early in the form of trotting poles, it can be brought in even before cantering, then you may be able to rid people of this idea. If they find, once they have had a taste of elementary jumping, that they really do not want to jump, they can stop then. But if you do introduce it very early, the jumps will have to remain very small for a long time.

You will have explained the rider's position when they first used trotting poles, so all you will have to do is raise the last pole to about fourteen to eighteen inches, remove the pole before the last, and they can go over it as a ride, in trot and well spaced out. Remind them to hold the neck strap with the inside hand and try to follow the movement of the horse's head. Once all the pupils are able to go with the horse easily every time, you can have them jumping individually. This way, the jump itself becomes part of a general exercise in control. Have the ride lined up in the centre of the school and ask each rider to take his horse out onto the track and trot on, over the jump, round the school, and over the jump again. By this means you should be able to teach each pupil to start riding again actively, the moment his horse has negotiated the pole. Be very firm about their not cutting the corners, especially the one after the jump; put an oil-drum or something similar in such a position that they have to go round outside it. If you are lax about this, you may end up with a group of riders who do a splendid approach to a sizeable jump, sit beautifully over it, but stop riding as the horse takes off and allow it to turn immediately on landing and rejoin the other horses. The reason for not allowing this is not only that you want accurate riding and obedient horses; you should avoid allowing the horses to turn in suddenly on landing because this unseats far more riders than the actual jump itself. Instil the habit of thinking ahead. Try and get your pupils to stop thinking about the jump the moment the horse takes off and think of where they will be riding next, be it merely straight on or over another jump. This is the basis of later ability to ride round a course of obstacles and, as I have said before, good habits cannot be formed too soon.

It is in the very early jumping lessons that your pupils should learn to keep their heads up and look straight ahead when going over a jump. So many people look down and this is one of the surest ways of getting into the habit of failing to start riding the horse again immediately on the landing side. Looking down can also lead to the habit of rounding the back as the horse takes off, but some people round their backs in the mistaken idea that they are leaning forward and remaining in balance that way. They do not, at first, understand that it is possible to get 'left behind' even though their head and shoulders are forward. Probably the best way to avoid this is to get them to hollow their backs on take-off, as well as pushing the chin slightly forward and the weight down into the heels. Try telling them to think, not of going *up* with their horse over a jump, but going *down* to meet the horse as it takes off, by closing the angle of hip and knee.

Another habit that should never be allowed to form is the one of resting both hands on the neck or withers, on take-off. Explain the natural movement of the horse's head and neck throughout the jump and emphasise the importance of the

. . . . this unseats far more riders than the jump itself . . . .

rider's hands and arms being independant. Pupils do not have to be very advanced to ride safely over a small obstacle with their reins knotted and their hands free, and this exercise is the best one to convince a rider that he does not need hands, to keep his balance over a jump. A pupil who has acquired the bad habit of actually resting his hands on the neck or withers should be asked to jump without reins frequently until he has cured himself. There is one way of preventing the habit forming, with beginners who adopt the position through a feeling of insecurity; tell them to hold the neck strap and, as the horse takes off, tell them to push the neck strap forward up the horse's neck. This builds up confidence and after a while they are able to convince themselves that they do not, in fact, need their hands to hold themselves in the saddle.

The current practice seems to be to introduce pupils to jumping via the jumping position on the flat and over trotting poles and to continue over small obstacles. Certainly this does teach the position but no novice rider can satisfactorily build up and keep impulsion when he is in that position on a lazy horse, so it really only works on a free-going horse. In other words, he cannot, in that way, learn much about riding an approach. The average riding school horse will only jump this way for a beginner if it is being ridden over the jump in a ride, not if it is being asked to leave the ride and go on its own. Because of this, I have found it more satisfactory to abandon the use of the jumping position on the approach after beginner-pupils have practised it in one or two lessons. I do not return to it until many months later, in fact not until the pupil is reasonable advanced and can ride a horse on the bit, in a balanced canter with plenty of impulsion and with his seat-bones just clear of the saddle; this, in any case, will probably coincide with when he becomes capable of riding the more free-going horses and is jumping bigger fences out of

. . . . in the mistaken idea that they are leaning forward and remaining in balance . . . .

doors. It may be difficult to learn to sit down in the saddle and push a sluggish horse into a fence, and then get the weight forward at the last moment to avoid getting left behind, but when they start to accomplish this successfully, your pupils will be beginning to turn into active, as opposed to passive, riders. I think it is much easier to graduate from sticky to free jumpers than vice versa. Anyone who can push a lazy horse over a fence with determination, will find no difficulty in fining down his aids when he starts to jump free-going horses. On the other hand, pupils who learn to jump by merely sitting on a horse and pointing it at a fence will be helpless when they are asked to ride a horse which, given the opportunity, stops in front of a fence.

When anyone who has learnt to jump in an indoor school jumps outside for the first time, he will probably find it much easier, though the additional space and the feeling of freedom does sometimes tempt people to go too fast and start their approach too far from the fence. It is as well to make your pupils do plenty of jumping out of a trot, when they first start to jump outside. Before you ask them to jump in canter, try to get through to them that impulsion is what is needed, not speed. You will no doubt have told them this, if their lessons started indoors, but they will probably need reminding. Most of your pupils will have watched the experts riding speed-contests on television and the first time you ask them to ride even a short course of, say, four or five fences, they may well appear to have slight delusions of grandeur. People almost invariably go much too fast, at first, consequently are not in complete control and fail to treat each fence as a separate exercise. It is almost as if they feel that once they start the horse going, by riding at the first fence with determination, all that will be necessary thereafter is to maintain the speed and aim the horse in the right direction. People can be a little hard to convince, at first, that speed is not required. You may be lucky in that, because of your pupil's poor control at speed, his horse will have taken him round, rather than over, a few of the fences and this should serve to prove your point that impulsion and control are needed, even if it does not do the horse any good.

Insist that in the early stages, when jumping a course of fences, they regard each one as a separate entity and go through the whole procedure of approach each time. Between each fence they should steady the horse with half halts to build up the impulsion again before riding the next approach. Months later, when they can do this effectively without any running out or refusals, they can start to develop a more fluent style of riding round a course.

Keep the fences small for a long time. So often you meet people who have been taken on too fast, simply because they have not made a habit of falling off; they may be able to stay on over about 3' 6" and not actually interfere with the horse but their style is all wrong and they are very stiff. Keep the jumps at 2' to 2' 6" until they can ride over them in an easy, relaxed manner every time, remaining balanced and close to the saddle; only then start to raise the fences. There is so much in the way of variety you can provide with low fences such as spreads, combinations, twisting courses and so on, that there should be no excuse for pupils getting bored because the fences remain very small.

Of course, if a jumping lane is available to you, make full use of it and give your pupils plenty of jumping in it without reins and stirrups, as soon as they are sufficiently secure in the saddle. Take advantage, also of small tree trunks and ditches and any other suitable obstacles you encounter when out hacking.

Chapter 16

CONCLUSION

One of the slowest things to come to a trainee instructor is confidence. Even if you are bothered by stage-fright each time you give a lesson, you must try to give an impression of being calm, confident and in command. If you do, this act will soon become a reality. Perhaps one of the best ways of doing this is to try to remember all the time that you know more than you pupils. Admittedly, if your chief instructor is standing in the wings to see how you get on, *his* presence will no doubt make you nervous. Try remembering that he is there because he wants to be able to give you guidance for future lessons.

Don't be too ambitious in the early stages. If you know that you will be liable to become tied in knots if you try to take a double ride, don't try it. Wait to do this until you are confident that your riders won't end up milling about in confusion, because you don't know your right from your left, or can't be sure of giving the orders in time.

Occasionally you may find you have someone in your lesson who is as capable and experienced as you are. This can be unnerving, even to a fairly experienced instructor. If this happens, concentrate on how his horse is going. You can see things he can't and there is no reason why you shouldn't, tactfully, help him get the best out of his horse.

There is a tendency, with trainee instructors, to see only the obvious. Sometimes an obvious fault, or faults, in a pupil is caused by something far from obvious, so always look for a possible root-cause, otherwise correcting one symptom may only produce another.

Lastly, try to *enjoy* teaching and don't be deadly serious all the time, or your lessons will be dreary affairs which your pupils won't enjoy either.

INDEX